BUI 6/18/14

MONSTER TRUCKS

Aaron Carr

www.av2books.com

LET'S READ
AV²
BY WEIGL™
ADDED VALUE • AUDIO VISUAL

Go to **www.av2books.com**, and enter this book's unique code.

BOOK CODE

X995496

AV² by Weigl brings you media enhanced books that support active learning.

AV² provides enriched content that supplements and complements this book. Weigl's AV² books strive to create inspired learning and engage young minds in a total learning experience.

Your AV² Media Enhanced books come alive with...

 Audio
Listen to sections of the book read aloud.

 Video
Watch informative video clips.

 Embedded Weblinks
Gain additional information for research.

 Try This!
Complete activities and hands-on experiments.

 Key Words
Study vocabulary, and complete a matching word activity.

 Quizzes
Test your knowledge.

 Slide Show
View images and captions, and prepare a presentation.

... and much, much more!

Published by AV² by Weigl
350 5th Avenue, 59th Floor New York, NY 10118
Website: www.av2books.com   www.weigl.com

Library of Congress Control Number: 2013936158
ISBN 978-1-62127-380-6 (hardcover)
ISBN 978-1-62127-386-8 (softcover)

Printed in the United States of America in North Mankato, Minnesota
2 3 4 5 6 7 8 9 0 17 16 15 14

032014
WEP060314

Project Coordinator: Aaron Carr   Art Director: Terry Paulhus

Weigl acknowledges Getty Images as the primary image supplier for this title.

MONSTER TRUCKS

CONTENTS

Monster trucks are big machines.
They look like pickup trucks
with huge wheels.

Monster trucks were first made from normal trucks. Parts were added to make the trucks bigger.

Monster trucks weigh about 10,000 pounds.

Monster trucks can be seen at shows like Monster Jam. More than four million people watch these shows each year.

Monster trucks often race at Monster Jam shows. They race around turns and over jumps.

Monster trucks also jump over cars.
The cars can be laid in a line
or stacked on top of each other.

Monster trucks are best known for their big wheels. These wheels are as tall as a person and as wide as a car.

Monster trucks use tires made for farm tractors.

Monster trucks have big, powerful motors. These motors have the power of 1,500 horses.

Monster trucks have a cab where the driver sits. The driver often sits in the middle of the cab.

Monster trucks can be dangerous. They sometimes roll over or crash. People should always be careful around monster trucks.

MONSTER TRUCK FACTS

These pages provide more detail about the interesting facts found in the book. They are intended to be used by adults as a learning support to help young readers round out their knowledge of each machine featured in the *Mighty Machines* series.

Monster trucks are big machines. They are massive trucks that are used for motorsports and entertainment. They are known for rolling over cars with their huge tires. The first monster trucks were made in the 1970s when Bob Chandler built the first Bigfoot. By the 1980s, people were driving monster trucks in motorsports events across the country.

Monster trucks were first made from normal trucks. The first Bigfoot monster truck was made from a 1974 Ford F-250. It had a bigger motor and wheels installed, and the frame was strengthened to support its large size. Bigfoot had 48-inch (122-centimeter) tires and weighed about 10,000 pounds (4,500 kilograms). Today, monster trucks are specially designed vehicles that have little in common with normal trucks.

Monster trucks can be seen at shows like Monster Jam. Each year, there are more than 100 Monster Jam shows. Thousands of people pack stadiums for these events. Monster Jam shows take place in different cities around the world. The average monster truck team travels 45,000 miles (72,000 kilometers) each year to attend these events.

Monster trucks often race at Monster Jam shows. The races feature two trucks driving at one time. The trucks race around an oval track side-by-side, going around turns and launching off ramps and into the air. The truck with the fastest time goes to the next round. The races continue until there is a single winner. The fastest monster truck speed on record is 96.8 miles (155.8 km) an hour, set by Randy Moore in 2012. This record was set on a track with no turns, called a drag racing track.

Pages 12–13

Monster trucks also jump over cars. Monster Jam shows have two kinds of events—racing and freestyle. In freestyle events, drivers get a set amount of time to show off their skills. They drive around the course jumping off ramps and driving over cars. The world record for the longest jump by a monster truck is 214 feet (65 meters). The record was set in 2012 by Dan Runte. The cars come from local junkyards. They are returned to the junkyards after the event.

Pages 14–15

Monster trucks are best known for their big wheels. Monster truck wheels are about as tall as a person and almost as wide as a car. Most monster trucks today use 66-inch (168-cm) tires. Monster trucks use tires made for large farm tractors. Each tire can weigh up to 1,000 pounds (454 kg). This adds too much weight to a monster truck, so part of the rubber tread is cut off the tires before they are put onto the vehicle.

Pages 16–17

Monster trucks have big, powerful motors. Monster trucks use the same motors used in smaller trucks. They are usually eight-cylinder, or V8, motors with some special changes to make them more powerful. The motors are equipped with superchargers to add more power. They also burn a special kind of fuel called racing alcohol. Racing alcohol produces more power than gasoline.

Pages 18–19

Monster trucks have a cab where the driver sits. Most monster trucks have the driver's seat in the middle of the cab. Sitting in the middle of the cab gives drivers a better view of their surroundings. The windshields of most monster trucks are made of a type of plastic called Lexan. If the windshield is scratched, the outer layer of Lexan can be peeled off to create a smooth, clear surface.

Pages 20–21

Monster trucks can be very dangerous. They are massive machines that can cause serious injury. Monster truck drivers wear fire-resistant suits, helmets, head and neck supports, and five-point seat belts. Each truck is also made so that the cab will not collapse in the event of a rollover. To protect the people watching the show, monster trucks are equipped with safety features called kill switches. These devices shut off the motor if the driver loses control.

KEY WORDS

Research has shown that as much as 65 percent of all written material published in English is made up of 300 words. These 300 words cannot be taught using pictures or learned by sounding them out. They must be recognized by sight. This book contains 53 common sight words to help young readers improve their reading fluency and comprehension. This book also teaches young readers several important content words, such as proper nouns. These words are paired with pictures to aid in learning and improve understanding.

Page	Sight Words First Appearance
5	are, big, like, look, they, with
7	about, first, from, made, make, parts, the, to, were
9	at, be, can, each, four, more, people, seen, shows, than, these, watch, year
11	and, around, often, over, turns
12	a, also, cars, in, line, of, on, or, other
15	as, farm, for, known, their, use
16	have
18	where
20	always, should, sometimes

Page	Content Words First Appearance
5	machines, monster trucks, pickup trucks, wheels
7	pounds
9	Monster Jam
11	jumps
15	person, tires, tractors, wheels
16	horses, motors, power
18	cab, driver, middle

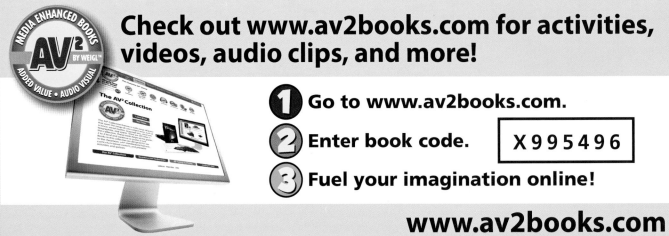

Check out www.av2books.com for activities, videos, audio clips, and more!

1 Go to www.av2books.com.

2 Enter book code. X 9 9 5 4 9 6

3 Fuel your imagination online!

www.av2books.com